Fee, Fie, Phonemic Awareness

Additional Resources Available From High/Scope Press

GENERAL READING RESOURCES

How Young Children Learn to Read in High/Scope Programs: A Series of Position papers

Children Achieving: Best Practices in Early Literacy
S. B Neuman & K. A. Roskos

Beginning Reading and Writing
D. S. Strickland & L. M. Morrow

Facilitating Preschool Literacy
R. Campbell

Learning to Read and Write: Developmentally Appropriate Practices for Young Children
S. Neuman, C. Copple, & S. Bredekamp

Much More than the ABCs: The Early Stages of Reading and Writing
J. Schickedanz

Starting Out Right: A Guide to Promoting Children's Reading Success
M. S. Burns & P. Griffen

PRESCHOOL READING

Educating Young Children: Active Learning Practices for Preschool and Child Care Programs (2nd Ed.)
M. Hohmann & D. P. Weikart

High/Scope Preschool Key Experiences Series: Language and Literacy Video and Booklet

Helping Your Preschool Child Become a Reader: Ideas for Parents

You and Your Child Parent Newsletter Series
12 titles: Young Children and Reading, Young Children and Writing, Young Children and Mathematics, Young Children and Art, Young Children and Dramatic Play, Young Children and Music, Young Children and Movement, Young Children as Family Members, Young Children as Communicators, Young Children as Decision Makers, Young Children as Challengers, and Young Children as Problem Solvers.

ELEMENTARY READING

High/Scope K–3 Curriculum Series: Language & Literacy
J. Maehr

Literature-Based Workshops for Language Arts—Ideas for Active Learning, Grades K–2
K. Morrison, T. Dittrich, & J. Claridge

Elementary Curriculum Video Series: Language & Literacy

Available from

HIGH/SCOPE® PRESS

A division of the High/Scope Educational Research Foundation
600 North River Street
Ypsilanti, MI 48198-2898
800/407-7377, FAX 800/442-4329
E-mail: *press@highscope.org*
Web site: *www.highscope.org*

Fee, Fie, Phonemic Awareness

130 Prereading Activities for Preschoolers

Mary Hohmann

Ypsilanti, Michigan

Published by

High/Scope® Press
A division of the High/Scope Educational Research Foundation
600 North River Street
Ypsilanti, Michigan 48198-2898
734/485-2000, Fax 734/485-0704
press@highscope.org

Editor: Nancy Brickman
Cover design, text design: Judy Seling, Seling Design
Cover illustration: Robin Williamson
Photography:
Gregory Fox Photography—7, 8, 12, 14, 15, 16, 19, 24, 27, 30, 35, 39, 40, 41, 44, 47, 49, 61
Patricia Evans—6, 25, 36, 51, 53, 55, 57

Library of Congress Cataloging-in-Publication Data
Hohmann, Mary.
  Fee, fie, phonemic awareness : 130 prereading activities for preschoolers / Mary Hohmann.
    p. cm.
  ISBN 1-57379-128-8 (softcover : alk. paper)
  1. English language--Phonemics--Study and teaching (Preschool)--Activity programs. 2.
Reading--Phonetic method. 3. Listening--Study and teaching (Preschool)--Activity programs.
4. Education, Preschool--Activity programs. I. Title.
  LB1050.34 .H66 2002
  372.46'5--dc21
                                        2002010588

Printed in the United States of America
10 9 8 7 6 5

CONTENTS

Chapter 2. Building Rhyme Awareness 19

Fee, Fie, Phonemic Awareness

INTRODUCTION

Research from around the world has shown that building young children's awareness of the sounds that make up words in preschool, kindergarten, and first grade can significantly influence their subsequent reading and writing achievement. *Fee, Fie, Phonemic Awareness: 130 Prereading Activities for Preschoolers* is High/Scope's **early childhood** answer to the national call for explicit, systematic instruction in phonological and phonemic awareness before children reach third grade. The activities in *Fee, Fie, Phonemic Awareness* provide over 20 hours of active small-group instructional experiences explicitly aimed at drawing three-, four-, and five-year-old children's attention to the sounds in words they are beginning to hear and explore. These word sounds include rhymes, alliteration, and the sounds represented by letters. Based on the 2000 report of the National Reading Panel, the Partnership for Reading (2001)[1] suggests that 20 hours of activities over the course of a program year is sufficient for developing phonemic awareness at this age. This book can provide you with more than enough such activities to meet this 20-hour standard.

Although these activities are designed as part of the High/Scope educational approach, they are suitable for any preschool program that strives to support children's letter recognition and awareness of the sounds in words within the broad context of child development. The activities are short (about 10 minutes each), self-explanatory, and enjoyable; and they require no special materials beyond what is normally found in an active learning preschool setting. Most are designed to occur in small groups—at planning, recall, small-group, snack, and transition times. These intimate settings insure that all children have the opportunity to wrestle with a beginning set of literacy ideas in the company of a trusted teacher and familiar classmates. Once exposed to these ideas, children tend to incorporate them into their ongoing exploration and play initiatives.

Phonological Awareness, Phonemic Awareness, and Letter Recognition

High/Scope supports the national call for literacy. We know that children's experiences with speaking, listening, reading, and writing in the preschool years lay the groundwork for reading success in elementary school. Moreover, learning to read exercises children's capacities for thought, curiosity, imagination, and empathy.

---

[1]The Partnership for Reading is a collaborative effort of the National Institute for Literacy, the National Institute for Child Health and Human Development, and the U.S. Department of Education.

By the preschool years, children's brains are organized for symbolic thought, so children are ready to begin to develop some of the abilities needed for reading. There are several keys that enable preschool children to unlock the door to fluency, comprehension, and interest in reading: trusting relationships, dialogue with empathic adults, and experiences with object exploration, representation (pretending, artwork, building), storytelling, books, and writing. The High/Scope preschool approach as a whole and the language and literacy key experiences in particular (see "High/Scope Preschool Language and Literacy Key Experiences" at left) provide children with these essential preschool keys to reading. In the process, children gain experience with another important aspect of literacy—the awareness of speech sounds, and in particular, *phonemic awareness.*

To describe how experiences with speech sounds affect children's developing literacy, it is important first to define some terms. Although you may have heard the terms phonological awareness and phonemic awareness used interchangeably, the terms have different meanings. *Phonological awareness* is the broader term; it refers to a set of abilities, one of which is *phonemic awareness.*

The word *phonology* refers to the science of speech sounds. *Phonological awareness* is the ability to recognize the sound structure of speech, that is, the ability to perceive word sounds and pronounce words and parts of words.

Children develop phonological awareness when they can hold speech sounds in mind. To be ready for phonological awareness, children need to be able to hear the specific sounds that make up a word and at the same time keep in mind the sound of the whole word. At ages three to four years, children are just developing the part-whole memory capacity necessary for phonological awareness. Around this time, children with a reasonable command of speech can hear and consciously isolate and say certain sounds in words. Specifically, the sounds in words they are attuned to are *rhymes* (word endings that sound the same, such as the -at sound in *cat, bat,* and *mat)* and *alliteration* (word beginnings that sound the same, such as the /b/ sound in *big, bad,* and *ball).*

By the age of six or seven years, children become capable of hearing and breaking words into their *phonemes*—the sounds of letters and letter combinations that make up a word. (See "How Phonological Awareness Develops" on page 5.) A phoneme is the *smallest unit of sound in speech.* Phonemes combine with one another to make syllables and words.

For example, the word *big* combines three phonemes, /b/, /ĭ/, and /g/. The word *chuck* also contains three phonemes, /ch/, /ŭ/, and /k/, even though it uses five letters, because a phoneme can be represented in print as a single letter like /p/ or as a letter combination like /sh/. Depending on who's counting, the English language contains 40–52 phonemes. *Phonemic awareness,* then, is the ability to recognize spoken words as a sequence of various combinations of these 40–52 sounds.

In preschool, children enjoy hearing and experimenting with rhymes and alliteration. Drawing attention to alliteration is one fairly natural way for adults to involve preschoolers with phonemes. Specifically, adults can encourage *phoneme isolation* ("Fee! That starts with the /f/ sound!") and *phoneme matching* ("Fee, fie, fo, fum! These words all have the /f/ sound at the beginning!").

Another aspect of early reading and reading readiness is learning the alphabet. In preschool, three- and four-year-old children are engaged in representing familiar objects and actions in a variety of ways, including writing. They see adults write, they examine text in books and in their surroundings, they learn to recognize and name familiar letters, and they take up writing themselves. After experimenting with the emergent forms of writing, they begin to write "real" letters, starting with the letters in their names and other personally significant words. As beginning writers, preschoolers also wrestle with phonemes as they say the sounds in words they are attempting to write (*"Mom—/m/"*).

The activities in this book enable preschool teachers to build children's awareness of the sounds that make up words as an explicit part of their ongoing efforts to encourage children's talk and fun with language. These activities also enable teachers to incorporate a systematic approach to alphabet learning into their ongoing focus on children's exploration, representation, and beginning writing. With the competencies gained through these experiences, children will be ready to tackle formal reading instruction in the elementary grades.

How Phonological Awareness (Awareness of Sounds in Words) Develops

Age three to five years—
Children can hear rhymes: mail, pail, sail.

Children can hear alliteration: fee, fie, fo, fum.

Age five to six years
Children can segment words they hear into chunks called **syllables**: din-o-saur.

Children can segment words they hear into chunks called **onsets** and **rimes**: /b/-oat, /g/-oat; /d/-ock, /l/-ock.

Children can identify different sounds at the beginnings of words (rock, sock).

Children can identify different sounds at the ends of words (stem, step).

Children can hear different sounds in the middles of words (dig, dog).

Age six to seven years
Children can hear, segment, and say phonemes in a word separately (/c/ /ă/ /t/).

Children can hear, delete, and move phonemes in a word (/t/ /ŭ/ /b/, /ŭ/ /b/, /b/ /ŭ/ /t/).

How to Use This Book

To familiarize yourself with this book, take a few minutes to skim through each of the five chapters to gain an overall sense of the types of activities offered. Each chapter begins with relatively simple activities and progresses to increasingly complex activities.

The activities in the first chapter, "Identifying Sounds," are a good place to begin. These activities help children attune their ears to everyday sounds. Listening to and identifying these common noises in their environment helps children distinguish the most distinct and familiar sounds and provides experiences they can build on as they begin to pick out the subtler sounds that go

Intimate small-group settings like this one allow children to wrestle with literacy ideas in the company of a trusted teacher and familiar classmates.

together to make up words. Once you have a sense of how well your children are able to identify sounds, you may want to begin interspersing early activities from the second chapter, "Building Rhyme Awareness," with later activities from the first.

Alternatively, since each chapter begins with repertoire-building and materials exploration, you may want to do the activities at the beginning of the first chapter the first week; the beginning of the second chapter the next; and so on, so that over the course of five weeks or so, you have started each activity strand. The next step would be to select and offer a series of the later activities from each chapter, and so on, so that you keep circling through each chapter at progressively more complex levels.

Whether you present the activities in order chapter by chapter, or work through the chapters in a circular fashion, it's important to keep track of which activities you are doing, how children are responding to them, and how you adapt them to your classroom.

There is no need to rush through these activities or to dwell on ones that children have already mastered. On the other hand, you and your children will want to return from time to time to favorite activities. You may also find it prudent to adapt activities for various purposes: to suit the particular interests of your children, to fit your daily routine, or to incorporate similar materials readily at hand.

While explicitly focused, the activities in *Fee, Fie, Phonemic Awareness* are also sufficiently open-ended to allow for a variety of responses and thus to accommodate a range of three-, four-, and five-year-olds who typically work, play, and develop understanding at their own personal rates. Further, some of the activities will overlap. For example, if the activity is guessing rhymes in a book by looking at the pictures, some children may guess the rhymes by looking at the first letter in the printed word and trying out its sound. During letter recognition activities, some children will want to explore letter sounds as they identify the letters visually. In any case, the main idea is to present these ideas to small groups of children, then support each child's response, pace, and level of understanding. In this manner, *all* the children in your class will learn and grow in their ability to hear the sounds that make up words.

Additional Resources to Use With the Activities

The "Helpful Resources" section at the end of the book provides additional materials to help you carry out the activities and record your progress. The Materials List on pp. 60-61 provides suggestions for materials by chapter. The list includes many everyday "found" materials and household objects, as well as a wide range of printed matter and print-related materials: books, magazines, and labels; writing and art tools and materials; and a variety of two- and three-dimensional letter sets. The Activity Log on pages 62–64 will show you which activities you have done and which ones to consider offering next. The language and literacy items from the High/Scope Child Observation Record for Ages $2\frac{1}{2}$–6 (COR) on pages 65–68 will help you profile individual children's knowledge of rhyming, alliteration, and letters. Using the COR items as directed will also provide you with anecdotal data to share with parents about their child's literacy strengths and accomplishments. The Phonics Fact Sheet for Parents that concludes the "Resources" section will help you answer parents' questions about phonics and reading in preschool.

Seeing their teacher write and trying out writing themselves are ways children learn the alphabet. After experimenting with squiggles and letterlike forms, they begin to write "real" letters, often starting with the letters in their names.

Most of the materials you will need to carry out the activities in this book are probably already part of your classroom.

A Note About Materials

The materials you will need to carry out the activities in *Fee, Fie, Phonemic Awareness* are included in the description of each activity. (They are also listed in the Materials List on pages 60–61.) Most of the materials called for are probably already part of your classroom. If they are not, they can be found in school supply catalogs, in your house, at discount stores, or online. One site we recommend for children's books is High/Scope (*www.highscope.org*). Another site we recommend for children's books, alphabet puzzles, and three-dimensional letters is Innovative Educators (*www.innovative-educators.com*).

▼

As you work through the activities in this book, remember that to develop phonological and phonemic awareness, children need to have a wide range of language and play experiences to communicate about and draw from. The more children talk and hear everyday sounds, the better they can hear and isolate sounds that make up words. They need to hear, say, and enjoy nursery rhymes and poems before they can tease apart rhyme endings and alliterative beginnings. They need to draw and scribble before they make letters. They need to use letters as everyday objects before they line them up to make words. And, they need to explore and play with objects to be able to interpret pictures and comprehend the written words that stand for them.

Related Research

Adams, M. J., Foorman, B. R., Lundberg, I., & Beeler, T. (1998). *Phonemic awareness in young children.* Baltimore: Paul Brookes Publishing.

Alegria, J., Pignot, E., & Morais, J. (1982). Phonetic analysis of speech and memory codes in beginning readers. *Memory and Cognition, 10,* 451–56.

Blachman, B. A. (1991). Getting ready to read: Learning how print maps to speech. In J. F. Kavanagh (Ed.), *The language continuum: From infancy to literacy* (pp. 41–62). Timonium, MD: York Press.

Bradley, L., & Bryant, P. E. (1983). Categorizing sounds and learning to read: A causal connection. *Nature, 301,* 419–421.

Byrne, B., & Fielding-Barnsley, R. (1995). Evaluation of a program to teach phonemic awareness to young children: A 2- and 3-year follow-up and a new preschool trial. *Journal of Educational Psychology, 87,* 488–503.

Calfee, R. C., Lindamood, P. E., & Lindamood, C. H. (1973). Accoustic-phonetic skills and reading: Kindergarten through 12th grade. *Journal of Educational Psychology, 64,* 293–298.

Campbell, R. (1998). *Facilitating preschool literacy.* Newark, DE: International Reading Association.

Cardoso-Martins, C. (1995). Sensitivity to rhymes, syllables, and phonemes in literacy acquisition in Portuguese. *Reading Research Quarterly, 30,* 808–828.

Castle, J. M., Riach, J., & Nicholson, T. (1994). Getting off to a better start in reading and spelling: The effects of phonemic awareness instruction within a whole-language program. *Journal of Educational Psychology, 86,* 350–359.

Center for the Improvement of Early Reading Achievement (CIERA). (2001). *Putting reading first: The research building blocks for teaching children to read.* Washington DC: Partnership for reading. Available at *http://www.nifl.gov/partnershipforreading/publications/recommended.*

Goswami, U. (2000). Phonological and lexical processes. In M. Kamil, P. Mosenthal, P. D. Pearson, and R. Barr (Eds.), *Handbook of reading research (Vol. III,* pp. 251–267). Mahwah, NJ: Lawrence Erlbaum Assoc.

Høien, T., Lundberg, I., Stanovitch, K. E., & Bjaalid, I. (1995). Components of phonological awareness. *Reading and Writing, 7,* 171–188.

Lundberg, I., Frost, J., & Peterson, O. P. (1988). Effects of an extensive program for stimulating phonological awareness in preschool children. *Reading Research Quarterly, 23,* 264–284.

National Reading Panel. (2000). *Teaching children to read: An evidence-based assessment of the scientific literature on reading and its implications for reading instruction.* Washington, DC: Author. Available at *http://www.nationalreadingpanel.org.*

Schickedanz, J. (1999). *Much more than the ABC's: The early stages of reading and writing.* Washington DC: National Association for the Education of Young Children (NAEYC).

Snow, C. E., Burns, S., & Griffin, P. (Eds.). (1998). *Preventing reading difficulties in young children.* Washington DC: National Academy Press.

Related High/Scope Publications

DeBruin-Parecki, A., & Hohmann, M. (2003). *Letter links: Alphabet learning with children's names.* Ypsilanti, MI: High/Scope Press.

Epstein, A. E. (2002). *Helping your preschool child become a reader: Ideas for parents.* Ypsilanti, MI: High/Scope Press.

High/Scope Educational Research Foundation. *High/Scope Child Observation Record (COR) for Ages 2½–6.* (1992). Ypsilanti, MI: High/Scope Press.

High/Scope Educational Research Foundation. *How young children learn to read in High/Scope programs: A series of position papers.* (2001). Ypsilanti, MI: Author.

Hohmann, M. (2002, March/April). Exploring the sounds in words—Phonological & phonemic awareness for preschoolers. *High/Scope Extensions.*

Hohmann, M., & Weikart, D. P. (2002). *Educating young children: Active learning practices for preschool and child care programs.* Ypsilanti, MI: High/Scope Press.

Ranweiler, L. (In press.). *Promoting literacy in the preschool classroom.* Ypsilanti, MI: High/Scope Press.

1

IDENTIFYING SOUNDS

The following activities encourage children to hear, isolate, locate, and name environmental sounds, instrumental sounds, and voices, and to hear and act on particular words and phrases. These activities attune children to sounds and lay the groundwork for hearing and identifying the more subtle sounds that make up words.

Explore Sound-Making Materials

1. **Everyday materials.** At small-group time, provide each child with a collection of common materials with noise-making potential, for example, wooden blocks, chopsticks, tin cans, metal spoons, keys on a ring, paper plates, cellophane, and newspaper. Ask the children to find out what kinds of noises they can make. As children experiment with the materials, move from child to child listening and talking with children about the sounds you hear. At the end of small-group time, have each child make a favorite sound before returning the materials to their containers.

2. **Outside materials.** At small-group time, go outside. Ask each child to find materials they can use to make noise and to bring these back to the small group. As children gather with their noise-making materials, listen to and talk with them about the noises they have found. At the end of small-group, ask each child to make the sounds he or she has found, then have everyone make their sounds together. At outside time ask children to search for other things outside that make sounds.

Listening carefully to voices, environmental sounds, and musical instruments like these maracas helps children hear and identify the more subtle sounds that make up words.

3. **Percussion instruments.** At small-group time, put a selection of shakers, drums, bells, tambourines, triangles, wood blocks, and clavés where the children can easily see and reach them. Ask children to select and try out the instruments to find out what kinds of noises they make. Move among the children listening and talking with them about what they are doing and hearing. At the end of the activity, have children close their eyes and play their instrument alone when they hear you say their name. Finally, remind children that the instruments they are playing will be in the music area and that they can play them at work time.

4. **Xylophones.** At small-group time, give every child a mallet and every one or two children a xylophone. Ask them to play and listen to the sounds they can make. Move among the children listening and talking with them about what they are doing and hearing. At the end of group time, try playing a note and seeing if the children can find the same note on their xylophones. Children can also take turns playing a note for others to find. Finally, remind children that the xylophones will be in the music area and that they can play them at work time.

Attend to Environmental Sounds

5. **Sounds you hear.** Throughout the day, comment to children on the distinctive sounds you hear:

    "I hear the rain on the roof."

    "That's a dog barking!"

    "That sounds like someone walking in high heels. I wonder who it is."

    "I hear blocks clattering down."

    "I hear someone singing."

    "I hear the water running in the art area sink."

    "I hear bells."

    "I hear a siren."

    "I hear the garbage truck."

    "I hear the door closing."

These children, their teacher, and a mom pause on their walk to listen to the sound of water trickling over stones and around logs in the stream.

6. **Sounds children hear.** As children pause to listen to something that catches their attention, acknowledge or ask about what they hear:

"Dan, what do you hear?"

"That was a pretty big bang of thunder!"

"It looks like the sound of all those marbles rolling off the table onto the floor surprised you, Alana!"

"You stopped to listen to Julie's guitar."

Identify Rest-Time Sounds

7. **Indoor sounds.** As children settle down for a rest, ask them to listen for a few a minutes and tell you what sounds they hear before falling asleep.

8. **Outdoor sounds.** During nice weather, open the door or the windows at rest time, or take cots outside on the porch or in the shade. Ask children what sounds they hear as they fall asleep.

9. **Taped sounds.** At the beginning of rest time, put on a tape of bird calls, water falls, chimes (or some other distinctive, soothing sound). Ask children what sounds they hear.

Identify Snack- or Meal-Time Sounds

10. **While eating.** As children eat, ask them what sounds they hear at their table. Ask them what sounds they hear at the table next to them.

11. **Before eating.** At the beginning of the snack or meal, as children are passing out cups, napkins, silverware or as the lunch cart is rolling down the hall, have children close their eyes and say what they hear.

Identify Sounds on a Walk

12. **Listening for sounds.** At small-group time, take a walk, listen for sounds, and talk with children about sounds they hear.

13. **Listening for and taping sounds.** At small-group time, before taking a walk to listen for sounds, ask children what they think they might hear. Take a tape recorder. Tape sounds the children notice. Later on at the next small-group time, play the tape and encourage children to identify the sounds they hear.

Identify Animal Sounds

14. **Live animals.** At small-group time, visit a place in your area where children can see animals up close and listen to the sounds they make, for example, a pet store, animal shelter, stable, farm, or petting zoo. Take photographs of the animals and tape-record the sounds they make.

15. **Animal photos.** At small-group time, distribute all the animal photos you took on your live animal visit. Play the tape of the animal sounds. Ask the children to talk about the sounds they hear and figure out which of the animals in the photos are making each sound. If the sounds on the tape are indistinct, ask the children to make the sounds of the animals in their photos.

16. **Toy animals at planning time.** At planning time distribute a toy animal to each child in your planning group. Tell the children that to decide whose turn it will be to plan, you will make a animal noise, like "Quack, quack." The person whose animal says "Quack, quack" will be the person whose turn it is to plan.

"Quack, quack!" Children hear the sound a duck makes "up close and personal."

17. **Toy animals at recall time.** At recall time, give each child a toy animal. Decide whose turn it will be to recall based on the animal noise you make. For example, you might say

    "The person whose animal says, 'Moo, moo,' tell us what you did at work time today."

18. **Animal photos and/or pictures at planning or recall.** A variation on the preceding two activities is to distribute pictures of animals instead of animal toys. Proceed with either activity as above.

19. **Made-up animal sounds.** At planning or recall time, distribute models or pictures of unfamiliar animals. Have each child make up a sound for his or her animal. Make a child-created sound to indicate whose turn it will be to plan or recall.

Locate Sounds

20. **At planning/recall time, finding who has the noisy box.** Gather a set of identical boxes, canisters, or containers. Inside one put a bell, marbles, stones, rice, or any noise-making material. Leave the rest of the containers empty. Seal

each container so they all look the same. Distribute the boxes at planning or recall time. To determine whose turn it will be to plan (recall), sing a song like "Row, row, row your boat, gently down the stream. Merrily, merrily, merrily, merrily, now it's time to plan!" During the singing, have the children pass their boxes around the circle. When the song ends, the child with the noisy box plans. Have the children figure out who has the box. Repeat until all children have planned.

21. **At recall time, finding the ticking clock.** Find a wind-up clock (or timer) that makes an audible ticking noise. At recall time, have all the children except the recalling child cover their eyes. Meanwhile, the recalling child places the ticking clock out of sight, somewhere in the room he or she worked during work time. When the recalling child returns to the table, have the rest of the children open their eyes, listen, and say where they think the ticking clock is located and therefore, where the recalling child played.

Identify Voices

22. **Work-time voices.** During work time, tape-record short clips of each child in your planning and recall group as they play. At recall time, start the tape at the beginning and ask the children to identify the first voice they hear. When they identify the child's voice, have that child tell something about his or her work-time experiences. Then all listen to and identify the next voice on the tape, and so on, until each child's voice is identified and each child has recalled.

During work time, tape-record short clips of children's voices like those of these two boys. At recall time, have children identify the speakers they hear on the tape.

23. **Outside-time voices.** At outside time tape-record short clips of each child in your planning and recall group. Play this tape for children at snack time. Ask children to identify the voices they hear.

24. **Field-trip voices.** On a field trip, tape-record children's voices and any distinctive sounds associated with the field trip. At small-group time, play the tape and ask the children to identify the voices and sounds they hear. Give children paper and markers and ask them to draw something about the trip.

Listen for a Word or Phrase

25. **One magic word.** As a transition, give the children a word to listen for. Tell them that when they hear that word, they can then go put on their coats, crawl to their planning table, or whatever is next in the daily routine. For example, you might say

> "The magic word is **caboose!** When you hear the word *caboose*, you can go get your coats. Once there was little train who was very sad because it didn't have a cabbage to carry. (pause) But it did have a box car that was full of lions! (pause) And a beautiful red caboose named Sniffy..."

The magic word to listen for in this child's story is "Help!"

26. **One magic word from a child.** After the children have played enough versions of the previous transition game to understand how it works, have a child pick a magic word for the others to listen for and tell a short story that uses the magic word.

27. **One magic word repeated twice.** Make the magic word a repeated word such as *beep-beep*. For example, you might say

> "The magic word is **beep-beep.** Not just one beep but two together, *beep-beep*. Once upon a time, a cat named Beep was sleeping in the sun on the back porch. 'Beep,' his mom called, 'wake up. It's time to catch a mouse for dinner.' Beep opened one eye and then fell back to sleep. Then 'beep-beep' went the…"

28. **Two magic words.** Make the magic word a magic two-word phrase like *noodle maker*. For example, you might say

> "The magic words are **noodle maker.** Not just *noodle* or *maker* but two words together, *noodle maker*. Once there was a man named Elvis, who wanted to make noodles for his wife. But he couldn't find the things he needed. He couldn't find the fresh eggs. He couldn't find the coffee maker. He couldn't find the noodle flour. He couldn't find the ceramic bowls. And the *noodle maker* was nowhere in sight…"

2
BUILDING RHYME AWARENESS

The activities in this section are designed to help children gain phonological awareness, that is, to hear sounds that make up words. Specifically, they encourage children to identify and isolate rhymes—word endings that sound the same—in real and nonsense words.

Build a Repertoire of Rhymes, Rhyming Songs, and Stories with Rhymes

29. Rhymes and poems. Recite and read rhymes and poems to children on a regular basis—at greeting time, snack time, small-group time, and rest time. Enjoy these rhymes and poems for their own sake. Keep track of the rhymes and poems your children know and enjoy saying together. Then, use these familiar rhymes and poems in the activities that follow in the rest of this chapter.

"Hickory, dickory, dare. The pig flew up in the air! The man in brown soon brought him down. Hickory, dickery, dare." These children are learning a new rhyme to add to their repertoire.

Sample Rhyme and Poem Collections

Mother Goose rhymes: Any collection that includes "Hey Diddle, Diddle," "Hickory, Dickory, Dock," "Higglety, Pigglety, Pop," "Humpty Dumpty," "Jack Be Nimble," "Little Boy Blue," "Little Jack Horner," "Little Miss Muffet," "Old King Cole," "Old Mother Hubbard," "One, Two, Buckle My Shoe," "There Was an Old Woman," "Wee Willie Winkie"

Anna Banana: 101 Jump Rope Rhymes by Joanna Cole, Alan Tiegreen (illustrator)

Animal Crackers: A Delectable Collection of Pictures, Poems, and Lullabies for the Very Young by Jane Dyer (editor and illustrator)

Confetti; Poems for Children by Pat Mora, Enrique O. Sanchez (Illustrator) (Short poems incorporate varying amounts of Spanish into the English text.)

Good Morning, Sweetie Pie: And Other Poems for Little Children by Cynthia Rylant, Jane Dyer (Illustrator)

Noisy Poems by Jill Bennett, Nick Sharratt (Illustrator)

A. Nonny Mouse Writes Again! Poems by Jack Prelutsky (editor), Majorie Priceman (illustrator)

Rooster Crows by Maud and Miska Petersham

Sing a Song of Popcorn: Every Child's Book of Poems by Beatrice Shenk De Regniers, and others

30. **Rhyming stories.** Read rhyming stories to children on a regular basis—at greeting time, snack time, small-group time, and rest time. Before reading a new story or book aloud to the children, read it first to yourself. Find the rhymes, which sometimes spread across multiple pages, depending on how the text and pictures are arranged. When children are familiar with these rhyming stories and books, you can return to them as needed when doing the rhyming activities that follow.

Sample Rhyming Stories

The Duchess Bakes a Cake by Virginia Kahl

Each Peach Pear Plum by Janet and Allan Ahlberg

The Grumpy Morning by Pamela Duncan Edwards

How Big Is a Pig? by Clare Beaton

Is Your Mama a Llama? by Deborah Guarino, Steven Kellog (illustrator)

I Went Walking by Sue Williams

Jamberry by Bruce Degen

Jesse Bear, What Will You Wear? by Nancy White Carlston, Bruce Degen (illustrator)

The Lady with the Alligator Purse by Nadine Bernard Westcott

Low Song by Eve Merriam, Pam Paparone (illustrator)

Luella Mae, She's Run Away by Karen Beaumont Alarcon

Madeline by Ludwig Bemelmans

Mouse Mess by Linnea Asplind Riley

The Napping House by Audrey Wood, Don Wood (illustrator)

The Owl and the Pussy Cat by Edward Lear

A Pie Went By by Carolyn Dunn, Christopher Santoro (illustrator)

See You Later, Alligator by Laura McGee Kvasnosky

The Seven Silly Eaters by Mary Ann Hoberman, Marla Frazee (illustrator)

Silly Sally by Audrey Wood

Ten Little Rabbits by Virginia Grossman, Sylvia Long (illustrator)

The Three Little Pigs by Paul Galdone

Time for Bed by Mem Fox, Jane Dyer (illustrator)

31. **Rhyming songs.** Sing rhyming songs and fingerplays with children on a regular basis—at greeting time, snack time, transitions, large-group time, and rest time. Keep track of the rhyming songs your children know and enjoy singing together. Then, use these familiar rhyming songs and fingerplays in the activities that follow in the rest of this chapter.

Sample Rhyming Children's Songs

Baa, Baa Black Sheep

Eensy, Weensy Spider

Jack and Jill Went Up the Hill

Rain, Rain Go Away

Ring Around the Rosey

This Old Man

Twinkle, Twinkle Little Star

The Wheels on the Bus

Sample Rhyming Song Books

The Erie Canal by Peter Spier

The Fox Went Out One Chilly Night by Peter Spier

Hush Little Baby by Sylvia Long

I Know an Old Lady Who Swallowed a Fly by Simms Taback

The Itsy Bitsy Spider by Iza Trapani

Miss Mary Mack by Mary Ann Hoberman, Nadine Bernard (illustrator)

Over in the Meadow by John Langstaff, Feodor Rojankovsy (illustrator)

The Seals on the Bus by Lenny Hort, G. Brian Karus (illustrator)

Skip to My Lou by Nadine Bernard Westcott

There Was an Old Lady Who Swallowed a Pie by Alison Jackson

Identify Rhyming Words

32. **Using the word *rhyme* while reading stories.** When reading or reciting rhymes and rhyming stories the children are very familiar with, pause to identify words that rhyme. Use the word *rhyme* to describe their common ending sounds. For example, as you say or read the nursery rhyme "Hickory Dickory Dock," you might say

    "Hickory, dickory dock. The mouse ran up the clock. Do you know what? *Clock* sounds like *dock.* They both end with the sound **-ock.** *Clock* and *dock* rhyme!"

    Or, as you read the storybook *The Three Little Pigs,* you might say

    "Little pig, little pig, let me come in. Not by the hair of my chinny-chin-chin. (Pause.) That sounds like a rhyme right in the middle of this story! *In* and *chin* both have the **-in** sound at the end, so they rhyme."

33. **Children finding rhymes.** Ask children to identify the rhyming words. For example, you might say

    "Little Miss Muffit sat on a tuffit. Do you hear any words that rhyme? (pause) Little Miss Muffit sat on a tuffit. Which words rhyme?"

Fill In the Missing Rhyme

34. **One missing rhyme.** When reading or reciting familiar rhymes and rhyming stories, pause so children can fill in the familiar rhyming word. You'll find that you naturally emphasize the first rhyming word. For example,

"Hickory, dickory **dock.** The mouse ran up the _____."

"Rain, rain, go **away.** Come again another _____."

"Run, run as fast as you **can.** You can't catch me, I'm the Gingerbread _____."

"A bed for fishing, a bed for **cats,** a bed for a troupe of _____." (From *The Bed Book* by Sylvia Plath)

35. **Two missing rhymes.** When reading or reciting familiar rhymes and rhyming stories, pause so children can fill in both familiar rhyming words. For example,

"Jack be nimble, Jack be _____. Jack jump over the candle _____."

Substitute Nonrhyming Words for Familiar Rhyming Words

36. **One new nonrhyming word.** When reading or reciting familiar rhymes and rhyming stories, change one of the rhyming words in line or phrase for to a non-rhyming word to get a reaction from the children. For example, you might say

"Jack and Jill went up the **road** to fetch a pail of water."

"Jack and **Jim** went up the hill to fetch a pail of water."

"Little Bo Peep lost her **dogs** and didn't know where to find them."

"Little **Miss Muffet** lost her sheep and didn't know where to find them."

When the children notice and object to the nonrhyming word, ask them what's wrong with it. Listen to their explanations. Generally they will note that the new word is not right because it doesn't sound right. Eventually, they will understand and say that it doesn't sound right because it doesn't rhyme. If they don't use the word *rhyme* when they explain this, use the word yourself in your conversation with them.

37. **New nonrhyming words from children.** When children are familiar and comfortable with this activity, and have a good grasp of words that rhyme, ask them to substitute a nonrhyming word for a rhyming one. For example, you might say

"Little boy blue come blow your horn. The sheep's in the meadow the cow's in the... Where could the cow be that doesn't rhyme with *horn?*"

Try out the line with each new nonrhyming word the children offer and note out loud that, indeed, it does not rhyme with *corn*. For example, you might say

"Let's try Jamie's suggestion, *mud puddle*. Little boy blue, come blow your horn. The sheep's in the meadow the cow's in the **mud puddle.** Nope! *Mud puddle* does not rhyme with *horn!*"

Substitute New Rhymes for Old

38. **New rhyming words.** Change the rhyming words as you read or recite familiar rhymes. For example, you might say

"Here's a way to say 'Hey Diddle Diddle' with different rhymes:

"Hey **dink dink,**

The cat and the **sink,**

The cow jumped over the **rock.**

The little dog laughed to see such a sight

And the dish ran away with the **sock.**"

As you talk with the children about "Hey Dink Dink," point out or encourage them to identify the new rhymes, in this case *dink* and *sink,* and *rock* and *sock.* Depending on your children, you may want to begin this type of activity by offering one new set of rhymes *(dink* and *sink)* on one day and adding the second new set of rhymes *(rock* and *sock)* the next day.

By substituting "toe" for "no," these children have changed the rhyming phrase "Oh, no! Where did she go?" to "Oh, no! Where's my toe!"

39. **New rhyming words from children.** Ask children for two words that rhyme. Then, use these two words as substitutes in a familiar rhyme or poem. For example, you might say

> "Let's think of two words that rhyme," to which, after some thought, the children offer *bam* and *ham,* and *boo* and *who.* You would reply: "Let's see what happens when we try *bam* and *ham,* and *boo* and *who,* in 'Hey Diddle Diddle.' Here goes!

> "Hey **bam bam**

> The cat and the **ham**

> The cow jumped over the **boo.**

> The little dog laughed to see such a sight

> And the dish ran away with the **who!**"

Do It When It Rhymes

40. **Name-and-word pairs.** At a transition time, provide a series of word pairs in which one of the words, a child's name, is always the same. Ask the children to act on the word pair that rhymes. For example, as a transition between large-group time and outside time you might say

This child offers a word that rhymes with Jota's name: "Jota, boata!"

> "When you hear a word that rhymes with your name, you can go get your coat. But watch out 'cause I'm going to try to trick you! I'm going to start with your name, Sam. Hat, Sam. (Pause.) Sun, Sam. (Pause.) Jam, Sam."

41. **Name-and-word pairs from children.** When children can play the previous game with ease, have them generate words that rhyme or don't rhyme. For example, at snack time you might say

> "I want to play the rhyming-name game at the end of large-group time today, but I need some help thinking of words that rhyme with your names, and some words that don't rhyme with your names. So, what's a word that rhymes with *Toyanna?*" The children offer *Boyanna.* "Okay, Toyanna, Boyanna. They sound the same at the end. They rhyme. Now I need a word that doesn't rhyme with *Toyanna.*" The children offer *raisins.* "Toyanna, raisins. They don't rhyme! Now I need another word that doesn't rhyme with *Toyanna.*" The children offer *computer.*

42. **Three pairs of words, all words different.** Provide a series of word pairs, of which one word pair rhymes and two do not, and all of the words are different. For example, as a transition between greeting circle and planning time you might say

> "When you hear two words that rhyme, like *goat* and *boat,* jump to your planning table. Okay, here are the words: Cat, pan. (Pause.) Hill, ball. (Pause) Clock, block."

43. **Word-pair variations.** As you play this game, vary the number of pairs of words you offer. Vary *when* you offer the rhyming pair as well, offering it first, last, or in the middle of the series, and changing the order with each new turn.

Find Objects With Rhyming Names

44. **One object.** For small-group time, collect a set of familiar objects and toys, including objects with names that rhyme like a chair and some hair, a slipper and a zipper, a pear and a toy bear. Put an item in a basket or bag for each child and spread the rest of the materials where all the children can see and reach them. Then, ask the children to each find something whose name rhymes with the item in their basket or bag. Materials might include blocks, rocks, socks, and clocks; hats, mats, cats, and rats; pans, fans, men, cans, and vans; shells and bells; books and hooks; balls, walls, and shawls; boats, goats, and doll coats; cars, guitars, jars, and stars; moons, balloons, loons, and spoons; nails, pails, and veils; keys, trees, and bees; shoes and glue; a house and a mouse; dogs and Lincoln logs. Talk with each child about the rhyming items he or she has found.

45. **Two objects.** Do the previous small-group activity, this time putting two items into each child's basket or bag. Ask children to find things that rhyme with the first object's name and things that rhyme with the second.

46. **Room search.** When children are familiar with finding rhyming objects, try this activity at small-group time. Give each child an object. Ask them to search anywhere in the

---

Recognizing Rhymes

Eli's grandad writes some poems for Eli. Over the weekend, he and Eli pick out several for his grandad to read on his visit to preschool. On Monday, as Eli's grandad reads the poems out loud at large-group time, the teachers notice the children giggling when they hear rhyming words at the ends of lines—*log, bog,* and *cog.* They also notice that one child, Rex, repeats some of the rhyming lines to himself. They realize that their children are responding to rhyming word endings in poems they are hearing for the first time.

room for another object whose name rhymes with their object's and bring it back to the small group. Have each child show and name their rhyming objects.

47. **Guessing objects with rhyming names.** At small-group time give each child an object. Ask them to search anywhere in the room for another object whose name rhymes with their object's and put the rhyming object in a bag. Once children have gathered back together, have them try to guess the rhyming object in each child's bag. For example, you might say

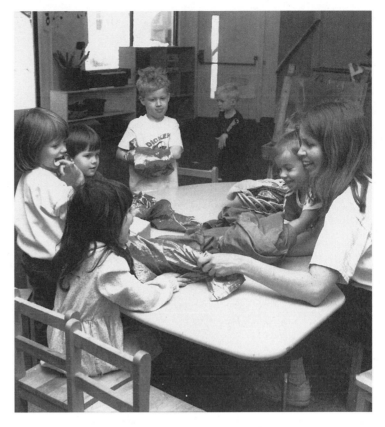

*"I feel something that rhymes with **clock**—a block!"*

> "What do think Ella has in her bag that rhymes with *moon?*" (A wooden moon was her original object.)

48. **Cleanup "I Spy."** At cleanup time play rhyming "I Spy" or "I See." For example, you might say

> "I see something that needs to be put away that rhymes with **willow.** What could it be?"

> "I see something that rhymes with **call.** What needs to be put away that rhymes with **call?**"

49. **Snack-time "I Spy."** At snack time play rhyming "I Spy" or "I See." For example, you might say

> "I see something that rhymes with **bug.** What do you think it could be?"

> "I see something that rhymes with **mink.** What do you think it is?"

50. **Child-led "I Spy."** Have children be the leaders in the rhyming game described above at cleanup and snack time.

Make Up Rhymes

51. Guessing what rhymes with... At snack or meal time, pick up an object at hand and see how many real and nonsense words the children can think of that rhyme with the object's name. For example, you might say

> "Everybody at this table has a cup. I wonder how many words we can think of that rhyme with **cup.**"

52. Rhyming puppet names, planning time. At planning time, give each child a puppet and ask the children to give their puppet a rhyming name (such as "Blake Snake"). Then, as each child's turn to plan comes up, ask the puppet its name and what its child's plan is. For example, you might say

> "This is my puppet Boggy Froggy. Think of a rhyming name for your puppet, then Boggy Froggy will ask your puppet about your plan."

After the children have had time to name their puppets, you might say to the first planner

> "Hello, I'm Boggy Froggy. What's your name?" Rachel, the child with the cat puppet might say, "Kitty Mitty." You might say to Kitty Mitty "Well, Kitty Mitty, what does Rachel plan to do today at work time?"

53. Rhyming puppet names, recall time. At recall time, give each child a puppet and ask the children to give their puppets rhyming names as above. Then, when it is each child's turn to recall, ask the puppet its name and what its child wants to say about work time.

54. Name rhymes. During transitions, make up rhyming phrases with children's names. For example, you might dismiss children at the end of the day by having each child supply a word or nonsense word that rhymes with his or her name:

> "Coat time for **Brian,** rhymes with _____ (lion, tryin', shian)."

> "Coat time for **Chris,** rhymes with _____ (miss, hiss, triss)."

Making Up Rhymes

One day at outside time, Rosie, a preschool teacher, sees Noel and Ellen sitting under a tree. "Two little girls," she says, "sitting by a tree. The first one said...." Rosie pauses to see what Noel and Ellen might say. "Whee!" says Noel. "The second one said..." continues Rosie. "I skinned my knee," Ellen offers. Here's the whole poem they made up together. Notice how Ellen brings the poem to a close by offering a non-rhyming line:

> Two little girls sitting by a tree.
>
> The first one said... "Whee!"
>
> The second one said... "I skinned my knee."
>
> The first one said... "What do I see?"
>
> The second one said... "She saw a key."
>
> The first one said... "Let's go get some French fries!"

If a child is not able to offer a rhyme, ask for suggestions from other children. If a child offers a nonrhyming word, acknowledge and accept it as such:

"**Jack** and **jump** have different ending sounds but they both start with the /j/ sound!"

55. **Outdoor rhymes.** Make up poems with children at outside time when they come to a pause in their play. For example, here are some possible opening lines:

(Christopher and Patrick) playing in the sand.

As they dig they….

Swing, swing, feet in the sky

When I swing, I….

Pulling the wagon all around

When we stop….

56. **Food rhymes.** At snack time, make up poems with children based on what they are eating or doing. For example, here are some possible opening lines:

Apples and pears

Let's….

When I drink juice

I….

Spreading spreading peanut butter

Makes me….

Find the Animal That Rhymes With...

At snack time, Sue, a teacher, reads *Whose Baby Am I?* (by John Butler). At the end of the book all the animal babies and mommies are pictured on two facing pages. Sue says, "I'm looking at the animal that rhymes with *Miranda* (the name of a child in the class)." The children guess *panda*. Sue says, "I'm looking at an animal who makes a sound that rhymes with *boo*." The children say, "Boo, whoo. The owl!" They continue this game through *peel* and *seal*, *chair* and *bear*, *Libra* and *zebra*, and *shmelephant* and *elephant*.

Look for Rhyming Pictures

57. **In storybooks at snack time.** Read a storybook with children at snack time. After completing the story, go back to some of the illustrations. For each illustration, give children a word and ask them to find an object or animal in the illustration that rhymes with it. For example, you might turn to picture of a barnyard and say

"I'm looking for an animal that rhymes with *wow*."

58. **In storybooks at greeting circle.** At greeting time, read a storybook with children. After completing the story, go back to some of the illustrations. For each illustration, give children a word and ask them to find an object or animal in the illustration that rhymes with it.

59. **In storybooks at small-group time.** At small-group time, meet in the book area. Ask each child to choose a book. Then, give each child a word (based on the pictures in that child's chosen book) and ask him or her to find a picture of something in the book that rhymes with the word. For example, if a child chooses the book *Good Night Moon*, you might give the word *home*, since the book includes a picture of a comb.

After their teacher reads them the rhyming story **Sleepy-O!** *(by Harriet Ziefert) the children search for the picture of something that rhymes with the word* **dreidel** *(a picture of a cradle).*

What Rhymes With Cat?

Rosie, a preschool teacher, shows the book *Rhymes with Cat*[1] (out of print, but still available at some discount stores) to her children at snack time. "All of the pictures in this book are things that rhyme with the word *cat*," she says. "Here's a cat on a...." She pauses. The children look at the picture and guess *mat*. "Here's a cat on a mat with a...." The children look at the picture and guess *hat*. "Here's a cat on a mat with a hat and a...." "Mouse!" Eli calls out. "Let's try *mouse*," says Rosie "to see if it rhymes with *cat*—cat, mouse." Eli and the other children hear right away that the two words sound different and say, "No, *mouse* doesn't rhyme with *cat*." Irene, another child in the group, offers the word *rat*, which everyone agrees rhymes with *cat*. The last picture includes a bat, which the children guess. Rosie and the children repeat this process with four more short books, *Rhymes with Cub, Rhymes with Cow, Rhymes with Hen*, and *Rhymes with Duck*. When they come to confusing pictures, they offer words and test each word against the word it's supposed to rhyme with. When they have exhausted their guesses, Rosie provides the rhyming word. For example, the children see a picture of a bear cub washing and offer *bath* and *wash* but know they don't rhyme with *cub*, so Rosie offers the word *scrub*.

[1]*Another series of books still in print that can be used in a similar manner are the* **Easy Words to Read Books** *(Jenny Tyler, series editor, Stephen Cartwright, illustrator). These nine short books include* **Big Pig on a Dig, Ted in a Red Bed, Sam Sheep Can't Sleep,** *and* **Goose on the Loose.**

60. In the *I Spy* books. At small-group time, give each child or each pair of children one of the *I Spy* books (*I Spy Little Animals, I Spy Little Bunnies,* and *I Spy Year-Round Challenger,* by Jean Marzollo and Walter Wick). Give each child a rhyme to hunt for. For example, you might say

"See if you can spy something that rhymes with *house.*"

Build Rhymes From Rhyme Endings

61. Guessing what rhymes with -ack. At transition times, give children a common rhyme ending, such as -ack. Ask each child for a word that ends in -ack before going to wash their hands, getting their coats, or whatever happens next.

Common Rhyme Endings

-ack	-ice	-ore	-ick	-ot	-ide	-ock	-ail
-igh	-eat	-ain	-ill	-ake	-uck	-ale	-in
-oke	-ug	-ine	-ame	-ing	-ump	-an	-ell
-ink	-unk	-ank	-ip	-ap	-ash	-it	-at
-ate	-op	-aw	-ay				

62. Thinking of words that end with -ate. At snack time, make a list of all the words children can think of that end with -ate. Choose a new rhyme ending another day. List those words. Put the lists together in a rhyming words book.

3

BUILDING
ALLITERATION
AWARENESS

The following activities are designed to build children's phonemic awareness of initial sounds in words when two or more words in a row begin with the same sound. These repeated initial sounds are called *alliterations.* These experiences provide opportunities for children to isolate and match phonemes at the beginnings of words as they recognize and create alliterative phrases.

Build an Alliteration Repertoire

63. **Alliterative phrases in stories, rhymes, and songs.** At greeting, snack, small-group, large-group, and rest times, read and tell stories, read and recite rhymes, and sing songs to children that include alliterative phrases such as the following:

Fee, fie, fo, fum	Fine feathered friends	Bye baby bunting
Clickity-clack, clickity-clack	Tom Tit Tot	Goodness gracious!
Clip, clop, clip, clop	Hip-hip-hooray	Meenie miney moe
Wee Willie Winkie	Peter, Peter pumpkin-eater	Trip trap, trip trap
Tic tack toe	Miss Mary Mack	King Cole
Snip, Snap, Snurr	Pease porridge	Topsy-turvy
Plink, plank, plunk	Hippity-hop, hippity-hop	Others...

Sample Storybooks That Include Alliteration

Alligators All Around: An Alphabet by Maurice Sendak

Alligators Arrived With Apples: A Potluck Alphabet Feast by Crescent Dragonwagon

The Baby Beebee Bird by Diane Redfield Massie, Steven Kellogg (illustrator)

Busy Buzzing Bumblebees and Other Tongue Twisters by Alvin Schwartz, Paul Meisel (illustrator)

The Duchess Bakes a Cake by Virginia Kahl

Jack and the Beanstalk by Steven Kellogg

Jack and the Beanstalk by Richard Walker, Niamh Sharkey (illustrator)

Mother Goose, any collection that includes "Bye Baby Bunting," "Diddle, Diddle, Dumpling," "Dickory, Dickory, Dare," "Goosey, Goosey, Gander," "Peter, Peter, Pumpkin Eater," "Simple Simon," "Sing a Song of Six Pence," "Wee Willie Winkie"

Miss Mary Mack by Mary Ann Hoberman, Nadine Bernard (illustrator)

Penguin Pup for Pinkerton by Steven Kellogg

Sheep on a Ship by Nancy Shaw, Margot Apple (illustrator)

Silly Sally by Audrey Wood

The Three Billy Goats Gruff by Mary Finch, Roberta Arenson (illustrator)

64. **Alliterative phrases in everyday conversation.** As you talk with children, use alliterative phrases from time to time. For example, you might say

> "Dylan's drawing dinosaurs!"

> "I'm crunching crispy crackers and soft cheese."

> "Goodness, gracious, golly! I've never seen such a long tunnel!"

Keep track of the alliterative phrases your children hear, say, and sing so you can use these familiar phrases in the activities that follow.

Identify Alliterations

65. **Pointing out common beginning sounds (initial phonemes).** After reading, reciting, or singing familiar alliterative phrases at greeting, snack, small-group, large-group, and rest times, pause and point out their common initial sounds to

At snack time, these children hear about the adventures of Milton the mischievous monkey. Later on, when they've heard the story several times, their teacher draws attention to the alliterative /m/ sound at the beginning of Milton, mischievous, and monkey.

children. For example, after reciting "Wee Willie Winkie" or retelling the English fairytale *Tom Tit Tot* you might say

> *"Wee, Willie,* and *Winkie* all start with the /w/ sound—/w/ Wee, /w/ Willie, /w/ Winkie."

> "I hear the /t/ sound at the beginning of *Tom, Tit,* and *Tot*—/t/ Tom, /t/ Tit, /t/ Tot."

66. Using the word *alliteration*. When children have had some experience hearing and identifying sequences of two or three words that start with the same sound, use the word *alliteration* to describe their common initial sounds. For example, you might say

> *"Tic, tack,* and *toe* all start with the /t/ sound—/t/ tic, /t/ tack, /t/ toe. That's called an **alliteration.** *Wee Willie Winkie* is an alliteration, too. Each word starts with the same sound—/w/."

Many children will enjoy the challenge of saying the word *alliteration* for its own sake—it's multisyllabic and full of sounds.

Recognizing Alliteration

At the small-group time the day after Eli's grandad reads his poems, the children in Rosie's small group make thank-you cards to send to him. Before they begin writing, they talk about the poems they remember and recite alliterative lines from one particular poem, "The Munchies." "Mice munching muffins" and "muffin munching mice" are two of the lines they recall. "You remembered the words that start with the /m/ sound," comments Rosie. "That's 'literation!" says Ellen.

Fill in the Missing Alliterations

67. Alliterative phrases from children. At greeting, snack, small-group, large-group, and rest times, read or tell familiar stories and rhymes that include alliterative phrases. Invite children to say them with you, or pause so the children can fill them in. For example, as you read or tell *The Three Billy Goats Gruff,* you might say

> "The first billy goat started across the bridge. How did his feet sound on the bridge?" (Pause for children's contribution.) "The second billy goat started across the bridge. His feet went _____."

José and the children come up with words that start with the /h/ sound like the sound at the beginning of his name: **hand, head, hot, José!**

Substitute New Alliterations for Old

68. Replacing the first sound (initial phoneme). At greeting, snack, small-group, large-group, and rest times, when reading familiar stories and rhymes that include alliterative phrases, substitute new beginning sounds in familiar alliterative phrases. For example, you might say

> "Here's a different way to say *Wee Willie Winkie* with the /m/ sound at the beginning: '**M**ee **M**illie **M**inkie ran through the town.'"

> "What if we said *Hip-hip-hooray* starting with the /b/ sound instead of the /h/ sound. We could say '**B**ip-**b**ip-**b**ooray!'"

69. New first sounds (initial phonemes) from children. Once the children have caught on to the idea of changing the initial sound of the alliterative phrase, see if they can offer a new beginning sound for a familiar alliterative phrase. For example, you might say

"What sound do you want to use for *Wee Willie Winkie* today instead of the /w/ sound at the beginning?" A child offers the /s/ sound. "Okay. Try it out. What would these words sound like with the /s/ sound at the beginning?" The children try out saying *See Silly Sinkie.*

Do It When You Hear the Alliteration

70. **Name-based alliterations.** During a transition time, ask children to choose an action. When they hear a word and a name that both start with the same sound (rain, Rex) they do the action. For example, after the children choose an action—jumping—you might say

> "Jump to your planning table when you hear someone's name and a word that starts with the same sound. Be careful. I might try to trick you! Here goes: Nut, Sue. (Pause.) Present, Crystal. (Pause.) Mop, Matt."

When playing this game, pair distinctive initial sounds like /s/ and /d/ or /b/ and /m/ rather than initial sounds that are very similar like /h/ and /p/, /k/ and /t/ or /tr/ and /ch/.

71. **Name-based alliterations from children.** After playing this game a number of times, invite children to be the leaders. Initially, they will probably be more apt at suggesting alliterative pairs than nonalliterative foils.

Tell Stories About Alliterative Objects

72. **Individual stories.** For small-group time, gather familiar objects and toys with names that begin with the same sound. Give each child a set of objects, and ask children to use their objects to make up or act out a story. After the children have had time to work with their collection, listen to each child's story. See if children notice that the objects they are using and talking about start with the same sound. If they do not, draw the sound to their attention. For example, you might say "Jonah, you made up a story about a bear, a ball, and a boat. *Bear, ball,* and *boat* all start with the /b/ sound!" Here are some sample object collections to consider for seven small-group times:

> /b/—bears, balls, boats, blocks, buttons, balloons, beans, bells, binoculars
>
> /c/—cats, cows, cars, cans, cardboard, cups, corks, cards
>
> /d/—dogs, deer, dough, dominoes
>
> /f/—foxes, feathers, fans, fences, flags, flamingos
>
> /m/—mice, maps, markers, marbles, magnets

/s/—spiders, stones, sticks, spools, straws, spoons, stamps, string

/t/—trains, tigers, tubes, tunnels, tents, taxis, Tinkertoys

73. **Group stories.** Combine several of the above sets of materials. Place the new set where all the children can see and reach them. Ask the children to find two (or three) things that start with the same sound. Have each child contribute to a group story about their alliterative objects. For example, your small-group story might develop along these lines:

> "Once there was a spider stone and a feather fan and a cat with corks on his ears."

74. **Stories from pictures.** Do the two small-group time activities just described. In place of objects, provide sets of photos or illustrations of familiar objects that start with the same sounds.

Play Alliterative "I Spy"

75. **At snack time.** Challenge children to find objects close at hand that begin with a particular sound. For example, you might say

> "I see something on the table that starts with the /b/ sound." The children offer *basket*. You reply *"Basket* starts with the /b/ sound. Can you think of any other words that start with the /b/ sound like *basket?"* The children offer *big* and *Brios*.

76. **At cleanup time.** As they tidy up, ask children to put away toys and materials whose names begin with a particular sound. For example, if the block area is littered with blocks, trucks, and tractors, you might say the following to a child:

> "Let's start with all the things that start with the /t/ sound."

77. **At recall time.** Begin recall by asking children to find something they used at work time and bring it back to the recall group. Select children to recall based on the initial sound of the objects they have in their hands. For example, you might say

> "Who has something that starts with the /b/ sound?" When the children identify the child holding the block or the boat, that person talks about what he or she did at work time.

78. **Recall-time variation.** At recall time, have children find something they used at work time, put it in a bag, and bring it back to the recall group. The child whose turn it is to talk about work-time experiences makes the initial sound of the object in his or her bag for the other children to guess. Once they do guess,

the child removes the object from the bag and recalls. For example, a child might say

"I've got an /m/ thing" or, "I've got something that starts with the /m/ sound." The children offer guesses. Finally, the recalling child pulls out a stone and says, "Magic stone!" "Yes," the teacher confirms, "*magic* starts with the /m/ sound. What did you do with your magic stone at work time?"

"Who is holding something they played with that starts with the /h/ sound?" asks this teacher at recall time.

Make Up Name-Based Alliterations

79. **At greeting circle.** Make up alliterative phrases that start with children's names. For example, you might say

"I'd like help thinking of some words that start, like Javon's name, with the /j/ sound." The children offer *Jack* and *jigsaw.* "*Javon, Jack, jigsaw.* Those are all /j/ words like *Javon.*"

"What are some /w/ words that start with the /w/ sound like Willa's name?" The children offer *wagon* and *window.* "*Willa, wagon, window* all start with /w/."

80. **At snack or meal time.** Decide who will pass out the cups, napkins, crackers, and so on by using name-based alliterations. For example, you might say

> "I'm wondering if there's a person with the /k/ sound at the beginning of their name like the /k/ sound at the beginning of *cup.*" The children offer *Caroline.* "*Caroline* and *cup* both start with the /k/ sound, so Caroline can pass out the cups today."

If no child in the group has a name that starts with /k/, begin the same way. Then, when the children determine that no one's name starts with /k/, offer another letter sound. For example, you might say

> "OK, no one's name starts with the /k/ sound. Could someone whose name starts with the /b/ sound pass out the cups? Whose name starts with the /b/ sound?" The children offer *Bing,* so Bing passes out the cups.

After each child makes up an alliterative name for his or her puppet, Frank Frog inquires about the child's plans for play. "What do you plan to do at work time today?" Frank Frog asks Dylan Duck.

4
RECOGNIZING LETTERS

The activities in this section are designed to encourage preschool children's early approaches to writing and to help them learn the names of the letters they are manipulating, forming, and writing.

Draw, Scribble, and Write Letters

81. At work time. Provide daily access to drawing and writing materials so children can draw and write wherever they are and whenever they want to, for whatever reason. Encourage children's interest in drawing and writing both as ends in themselves and as ways to carry out other plans and play.

82. During pretend play. At work time provide writing materials children may want to include in their pretending. For example, provide clipboards, markers, pencils, pens, paper, cardboard, notebooks, tablets, scratch pads, envelopes, planners, calendars, and receipt books for children to write signs, menus, shopping lists, prescriptions, appointments, tickets, schedules, phone messages, orders, bills, receipts, letters, invitations, and so forth during pretend play. Observe children in their play and look for opportunities to

Writing on note pads and clipboards plays a vital and enjoyable role in this play scenario!

support their use of writing to carry out the story line they have established. For example, if you are pretending to be a patient, you might say

> "Doctor, please write me a prescription for the medicine that will help my broken leg." When the "doctor" writes the prescription and gives it to you, find out from the doctor what it says. For example, you might say "Doctor, I can't read this without my glasses. Would you read it to me?"

Anticipate and support a range of writing styles—drawing, squiggles, letterlike forms, actual letters, and words—in any combination. When the children's writing includes recognizable letters, refer to them by name. For example, you might say

> "Oh yes. I see the *W* for *water*. Drink lots of water! I'll do that so my leg will get better!"

83. **At outside time.** Provide children with writing materials such as sidewalk chalk, paint, and water. Observe children as they use these materials in their play and look for opportunities to support their writing. For example, if children are drawing on the walkway with chalk, you might draw alongside them, print your name next to your drawing, watch to see if and how children add their names or other writing to their drawings, or ask if they would like to write their names. When the writing includes letters, refer to them by name.

84. **At planning time.** Give children markers and paper (single sheets, blank books, notepads, or one big group-sized piece). Ask children to write down what they plan to do at work time. Anticipate and support a range of writing styles—drawing, squiggles, letterlike forms, actual letters, and words—in any combination. Have each child read his or her plan to you. Refer by name to recognizable let-

Writing at Recall Time

At recall time, Rosie spreads out butcher paper and asks the children to draw something they did at work time. When Ellen finishes her drawing of herself painting at the easel, Rosie asks if she can write the name of the interest area where she worked. Ellen gets the word box, and copies the words *ART AREA* next to her drawing. "Oh," says Rosie. "I see you have written the letters *A, R, T* for *art*, and *A, R, E, A* for *area*. You painted in the art area!" Other children follow her lead, using the cards in the word box to write the names of the areas they worked in. Rosie notes that some children write the letters in conventional order. Others write the first letter first, the second letter second, and so forth, but place them wherever they fit on their drawings (as in Douglas's drawing, below).

ters when they occur. Repeat this activity several times a month. Over the course of the year, note the progress children make in writing actual letters.

85. **At recall time.** Give children writing materials. Ask them to write down what they did at work time. Have each child read what she or he has written. Refer by name to any recognizable letters the child writes. Repeat this activity several times a month.

86. **At small-group time, cards.** Give children paper, envelopes, and markers. Ask them to make greeting cards. For example, you might say

> "Here are some materials to write cards for your mom or your grandma. When your card is done, write the name of the person you want to give the card to on the envelope."

Anticipate and support a range of writing styles—drawing, squiggles, letterlike forms, actual letters, and words—in any combination. When the children's writing includes recognizable letters, refer to the letters by name.

87. **At small group time, more cards.** Over the course of the year, repeat this small-group-time activity to create thank-you cards, birthday cards, we-miss-you cards, holiday cards, invitations, get well cards, hello cards, welcome cards, and so on, as the occasion arises. Vary the kinds of paper, writing tools, and envelopes. Note the progress children make in writing actual letters.

88. **After a field trip.** Give children drawing and writing materials. Ask them to draw and write about what they did, saw, and experienced. For example, you might say

> "Here are some materials for you to write and draw about what you saw today at the house-building site."

Writing Messages

At small-group time, Sue gives her children pencils, blank index cards, and envelopes. "Yesterday," she says, "Micala made a greeting card for her mom and her grandma. I thought you might like to make some cards for people in your family or for people you know." As the children work on their cards, they write in a variety of ways: some children make scribbles; some write random letters; others write conventionally: *MOM, DAD, JORDAN AND DAD.* Children also pass their cards back and forth for others to look at or to copy the spelling of *MOM* or *DAD.*

Have the children read what they have written to you or to the whole group. Anticipate and support a range of writing styles—drawing, squiggles, letterlike forms, actual letters, and words—in any combination. When the children's writing includes recognizable letters, refer to the letters by name. ("I see you wrote the letter *H* for house.")

Identify Three-Dimensional Letters

89. **At work time.** Provide daily access to three-dimensional letters made of plastic, wood, wire, sandpaper, metal, sandstone, or popsicle sticks. Three-dimensional letters permit children to manipulate and explore letter forms, to feel the shape of each letter, and to use these letters as needed to carry out other plans and play. As children trace around, print with, sort, and arrange three-dimensional letters, refer to the letters they are handling by name. For example, you might sit next to a child who is looking at some letters she has traced and say

> "Oh, Jasmine, I see you have traced the *J* and the *S*."

90. **At small-group time, 12 letters.** Give each child a bag or basket of 12 or more three-dimensional letters to dump out, handle, build with, sort, arrange, and talk about. To begin, you might say

> "Here are some letters. See what you can do with them."

Large wooden three-dimensional letters allow children to handle, feel, sort, and arrange the alphabet letter by letter.

As the children work with their letters, watch, listen, and talk with individual children about what they are doing; make note of the letter names each child uses; and use the letter names yourself as part of the conversation. At the end of group time, put a letter down where all the children can see it. For example, put a *D* in the middle of the table. Have the children sort all their *D*'s into one pile, then put the pile of *D*'s into the storage container. Repeat this process with the letters the children know, then ask for all the rest of the letters in one big pile.

Identifying Three-Dimensional Letters

Linda knows that all the children in her small group can identify the letters *O, S, M,* and *X*. So, she includes these letters plus ten additional letters in each child's basket. "I'm wondering," Linda says, "who can find the letter *O* in their basket." She watches, listens, and converses with children as they hunt for and help one another find their *O*'s and then go on to play with and talk about the rest of the letters. At the end of small-group time she says, "Since it's almost time for outside time, find your letter *X* and see if you can use the *X* to help you put all your letters back in your basket."

91. At small-group time, known and unknown letters. Give each child a bag or basket of 12 or more three-dimensional letters. In each child's set, include the letters you know the child can identify by name and some letters the child may not know. Observe how the children explore their letters, and talk with individual children about how they are using the letters. Keep track of the letters each child names, and be sure to talk about letter names yourself. You may also want to provide children with paper and markers for tracing their letters.

92. At small-group time, letters in name. Give each child a set of 12 or more three-dimensional letters. In each child's set, include the letters in the child's name and a card bearing the child's name in print the same size as the three-dimensional letters. Instead of a card, you could include the child's nametag and letter link. (See *Letter Links: Alphabet Learning With Children's Names,* DeBruin-Parecki & Hohmann, 2003). To begin the small-group you might say

Nametag

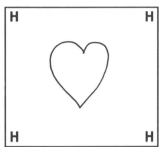

Letter link

> "Today in your baskets you have all the letters in your name. See if you can find the letters in your name in your basket."

As the children work, observe and listen to them, and talk with them about their play with the letters. Make note when children mention specific letters. As you talk with each child, say letter names yourself, repeating the letters in the child's name. You may also want to provide children with clay or dough for printing with their letters or for rolling and laying on top of their letters.

93. At small-group time, alphabet puzzles. Give each child or each pair of children an empty alphabet puzzle form and the letters that fit in it. Ask the children to fill in their puzzles. As the children work with their letter puzzles, observe and talk with them as in the previous activities, using letter names as a natural part of the conversation. Listen for the ways children talk about letters and note which letters each child can name. When children finish a puzzle they may want to trade puzzles with another child or pair.

Letters at Work Time

After several letter-focused small-group times, Linda notices that children are using the three-dimensional letters as props in their work-time plans and play ("Let's get the *O* for a bracelet"). She also observes them using the letters to convey messages (Brianna puts the wooden letters *N B* on her block house to stand for "No Boys") and to refer to as they are writing their own letters in signs and messages (Crystal finds and arranges the plastic letters *POP,* then traces them on the birthday card she's making).

94. **At snack time, alphabet pretzels.** Serve alphabet pretzels at snack time. As the children examine, sort, and eat their letters, watch, listen, talk with individual children about what they are doing, make note of the letter names each child uses, and use the letter names yourself as part of the conversation.

Make Three-Dimensional Letters

95. **At small-group time, clay or dough.** Spread out a set of three-dimensional letters where all the children can see and reach them. Then give each child clay or dough and ask them to use the clay or dough in some way to make letters. For example, you might say

> "Here is some clay. See how you can use your clay to make some letters. I put the letters out on the table to help you think of letters you'd like to make."

As the children roll the clay, form letters, or print in the clay with the three-dimensional letters, watch, listen, talk with individual children about what they are doing, make note of the letters children make and name, and use the letter names yourself as part of the conversation.

96. **At small-group time, wire.** Do the above small-group time using wire in place of clay or dough.

97. **At small-group time, pipe cleaners.** Do the above small-group time using pipe cleaners in place of clay or dough.

98. **At small-group time, sand.** Do the above small-group time outside, in the sand box if you have one. Otherwise, do it in any comfortable spot. Ask the children to make letters using sand, grass, sticks, stones, or nuts, or any combination of these materials.

*Natalie talks to her teacher about the "stand-up **n**'s" she made by rolling and bending small pieces of clay and pressing the ends onto her paper.*

Type and Print Letters

99. **At work time.** Provide daily access to sturdy working typewriters, letter stamps and ink pads, and, if you have computers in your classroom, to preschool word-processing programs and drawing programs that allow children to add conventional print to their drawings.

100. **At small-group time, computers and/or typewriters.** Open a children's word-processing program on each computer and meet in the computer area. Ask pairs of children to type letters and words they know. If there are more children than can sit together at the computers, have the rest of the children type on sturdy working typewriters. Each time you do this small-group activity, switch the children who last worked on a computer to a typewriter, and vice versa. If you do not have computers, use typewriters or a combination of typewriters and letter stamps and ink pads. As the children type and print letters, watch, listen, talk with individual children about what they are doing, make note of the letters children make and name, and use the letter names yourself as part of the conversation.

One way to type is to press the keys with your fingers and watch to see which letters come up on the paper! These boys later take their "letter paper" back to their small group to show and discuss the letters they made.

101. **At small-group time, letter stamps.** At small-group time, give children letter stamps, ink pads, paper, markers and envelopes and ask them to make greeting cards.

Sort and Arrange Letter Blocks, Tiles, and Cards

102. **At work time.** Provide access to letter blocks, letter tiles, and decks of letter cards. Watch to see how children use these materials. Play games following the rules children make up (and change) as they play! For example, children may play Memory by turning all the tiles or cards face down, then turning up as many as it takes to find a match. If a game of Scrabble is available, they will take great interest in lining up the letters in the squares. Their goal may be to fit all the letter tiles on the board without regard to spelling or length.

103. At small-group time, letters for each child. Give each child some letter blocks and letter tiles. In each child's set include the letters in the child's name, along with some other letters. As an opening statement you might say

"Here are some letter blocks and letter tiles. See what you can do with them."

As the children stack, line up, and sort their letters and tiles, watch, listen, talk with individual children about what they are doing, make note of the letters children make and name, and use the letter names yourself as part of the conversation.

104. At small-group time, letter search with blocks and tiles. Put the entire large collection of letter blocks and letter tiles where all the children can easily see and reach them. Ask them to find certain kinds of letters, for example, their favorite letters; a letter in their name; two letters that are the same; two letters that go together in some way (any reason the child offers is appropriate). Ask one of the children to suggest what kinds of letters they will be looking for. Throughout this activity, converse with children about the letters they are selecting. Refer to the letters they choose by name.

105. At small-group time, letter search with letter cards. Repeat the previous activity using letter cards in place of letter blocks and tiles.

Identify Letters in Print

106. At snack time. Read an alphabet picture book to children. As you read each alphabet letter, point to it. For example, as you read *"A is for alligator,"* point to the letter *A*. After reading about several letters, point to the next letter and pause so the children have a chance to name the letter and also identify the picture. Over the course of time, read a variety of alphabet books with children in this manner so they can see that alphabet letters in text can vary in size and style.

Sample Alphabet Books

The Alphabet/El Alfabeto by Gladys Rosa-Mendoza

ABC for You and Me by Meg Girnis

ABC T-Rex by Bernard Most

Alphabet Under Construction by Denise Fleming

Chicka Chicka ABC by Bill Martin, Lois Ehlert (illustrator)

Eating the Alphabet by Lois Ehlert

Flora McDonnell's ABC by Flora McDonnell

Into the A, B, Sea: An Ocean Alphabet by Deborah Lee Rose

Miss Spider's ABC by David Kirk

*As these children work on an alphabet book, some children draw the picture first, for example, a fire, and then add the letter **F**. On the **S** page already in the binder, in addition to the letter **S** and the accompanying picture, the child had the teacher write a further explanation: "Singing. Sing to the baby."*

107. At small-group time, making alphabet books. When children are familiar with alphabet books and how they work, provide paper and markers or crayons for children to make pages for their own alphabet book. For example, you might say

> "Today, let's try making our own alphabet book. Choose a letter, write it on your page, and then draw a picture of something that starts with that letter."

At the end of small-group time, assemble all the pages the children have made and read them. If some of the letters are repeated, read both *M* pages, for example, in a row. Decide with the children which pages are missing and make a plan to make those pages at the next small-group time(s).

108. At small-group time, making name-based alphabet books. Make an alphabet book based on the children's names, for example, *A* is for *Alana, B* is for *Ben.* Have children find their own photographs from a set you have taken, tape or paste them to a sheet of paper, then write or copy their name and the first letter of their name. When children have finished their pages, assemble all the pages in order and read them together. You may end up with multiple pages for some letters and blank pages for others. Make a plan with children about what to put on the blank pages. Complete the blank pages at another small-group time.

109. **At small-group time, identifying outdoor print.** At small-group time, take a walk around the block to look for letters—on signs, license plates, posters, storefronts, sidewalks. Talk with children about the letters they see. Take photographs for children to revisit at another small-group time once they are printed or developed.

110. **At small-group time, cutting out and saving letters.** At small-group time, place within children's sight and reach a collection of print materials with fairly large type, for example, newspaper headlines, magazine covers, advertisements, food labels. Give each child scissors and an envelope or small box for letter storage. Ask children to cut out letters and store them in their letter box or envelope. As children work, converse with them about the letters they are choosing and cutting out. At the end of small-group time, have children show and talk about some of the letters they have cut and saved. Ask them what they might want to do next with their letters (at home, at work time, or at the next small-group time).

111. **At small-group time, using cut-out letters.** At small-group time, have the children use their cut-out letters (see previous small-group activity) in the ways they suggested, for example, to paste on a piece of paper, to make their names, to paste on a card. Converse with each child about what he or she is doing, referring to the letters by name.

5
BUILDING LETTER-
SOUND AWARENESS

The following activities are built around preschool children's approach to noticing, forming, and writing letters and words, and are designed to help children associate letter sounds with the letters and words they are making and encountering.

Sound Out Letter Strings and Combinations

112. **At work time.** Both at work time and throughout the day, when a child writes a random string of letters and asks you "What word is this?" pronounce the "word" as written by making the sound of each letter. For example, if a child writes *DRSTLM* and asks, "What does this say?" you might say

> "Well, this word sounds like /d/ /r/ /s/ /t/ /l/ /m/: **drstlm!**"

Enjoy the word the child has created.

113. **At small-group time, random letter-block trains.** Give each child a set of four or five letter blocks, one triangle-shaped block (from another block set), and a piece of cardboard a little longer and wider than the block set.

This child has made a very long string of letters. It will be a challenge for José to sound it out.

Ask children to arrange their blocks on the cardboard to make a "word train." Then, visit each child, point to each letter block in order, and sound out the name of his or her train. For example, you might say something like this about a child's train:

"Jonas, your train says /m/ /ō/ /t/ /s/ /p/, **motsp!** Here comes the **motsp** train!"

114. At small-group time, selected letter blocks. Do the above small-group activity, this time giving each child a small set of letter blocks that includes a consonant pair and a vowel pair, for example, two *D*'s and two *A*'s.

115. At small-group time, letters-in-name block trains. Do the above small-group time, giving each child the letters in his or her name. If the child arranges letters in another order, sound out the word the child has created. For example, you might say

"Devon, your train says /v/ /ĕ/ /ŏ/ /n/ /d/, **veond!**"

On the other hand, if the child arranges the letters in the order of his name, you might say

"Your train says /d/ /e/ /v/ /ŏ/ /n/, **Devon!**"

116. At small-group time, random letter-block fences. Give each child some small toy farm animals. Place a good supply of letter blocks and/or letter tiles where children can easily see and reach them. Ask the children to build some letter fences for their animals using the blocks and tiles. As the children finish their fences, move from child to child, and sound out the word or words along each child's fences. For example, you might say

"Heather, you have all the chickens inside a fence that says /f/ /s/ /ŏ/ /k/ /z/ /w/, **fsokzw,** and /g/ /b/ /r/ /ĭ/ /d/ /ō/, **gbrido!**"

> **Connecting Sounds to Letters**
>
> At small-group time, as the children in Sue's group work with plastic letters, Rex arranges a *V* next to an *O* and says to Sue, "Look! *V* and *O!*" "*V* and *O*," says Sue. "They make the sounds /v/ and /ō/—vo!" At the other end of the table, Irene tries out Rex's idea. She puts together the letters *Z* and *O* and says, "/z/ /ō/—zo!"

Connect Sounds to Letters Children Use to Stand for Words

117. At work time. At work time and throughout the day, when a child writes a word using initial letters to represent whole words, comment on the sounds of these letters. For example, if a child writes *HB* and reads "Happy birthday," you might say

"I see how you wrote 'happy birthday'! You wrote the *H* for the /h/ sound at the beginning of *happy,* and *B* for the /b/ sound at the beginning of *birthday."*

118. **At small-group time, magnetic letters.** Give each child a metal tray, cookie sheet, or small cake pan and a set of 13–26 magnetic letters. Ask each child to write a message using the magnetic letters. When children have written their messages, ask each child to show his or her message for the other children to read, and then to read the message to the whole group. When children use letters to stand for whole words, comment on the sound the letter makes in the words. For example, if a child writes "I LV CA" and reads this as "I love cake," you might say

> "I see how you wrote that! You used an *I* for *I,* an *L* for the /l/ sound and a *V* for the /v/ sound in *love,* and a *C* for the /k/ sound and an *A* for the /ā/ sound in *cake!* You wrote the message 'I love cake'!"

*Gabriella places her umbrella symbol under the letter G and a photograph of herself at play. "Gabriella starts with **G**— /g/, Gabriella," her teacher says.*

119. **At small-group time, erase board.** Do the above message-writing activity, giving each child a dry-erase board and markers or a magic slate and stylus.

120. **At small-group time, letter stickers.** Do the above message-writing activity, giving each child letter stickers and paper or card stock.

Link Letter Sounds With Letter Names When Asked to Spell

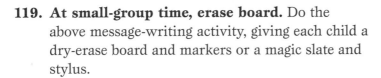

121. **Beginning and ending sounds in words.** At work time and throughout the day, when a child asks you how to spell a word, make the beginning and ending sounds of the word as you spell. For example, if a child asks you to spell *Daddy,* you might say

> "It starts with the sound *dă,* that's D, A. (Pause for the child to write.) Then it ends with the sound *dē,* that's D, D, Y. (Pause while the child writes.) You've written the word *daddy,* D, A, D, D, Y!"

122. **Remaining sounds in words.** At work time and throughout the day, when a child asks you about a sound in a word, make the sound needed, then pause to give the child a chance to figure out a way to write that sound. For example, if a child makes a *D* and says "What's next in *dog?*" you might say

"It's -og. How could you write the sound -og?"

The child may then write *G*, *AWG*, or *OG* to complete the word. If the child has no idea about what to write, supply the letters:

"You write -og in *dog* as *O, G.*"

123. **At planning time, words and pictures.** Ask children to draw a picture of what they plan to do and write a word that goes with the picture. If a child asks for spelling help, use letter sounds and letters as described above. As you talk with each child about his or her picture and plan, connect the letter sounds to the letters children use to stand for words.

124. **At recall time, words and pictures.** Ask children to draw a picture of something they did at work time and write a word that goes with the picture. If a child asks for spelling help, use letter sounds as in the previous activities. As you talk with each child about his or her picture and plan, connect the letter sounds to the letters children use to stand for words.

125. **At snack time, food words.** Ask children how they would write the name of whatever they are eating. Write down and note the letter sounds in children's spelling suggestions. For example, if the children are spreading peanut butter on crackers, you might ask them how they would write down the words *peanut butter* or the word *cracker*. After a child has written *PE NT BTR*, you might say

"OK, we have *P* for the /p/ sound, *E* for the /ē/ sound, *N* for the /n/ sound, *T* for the /t/ sound…"

Sounding Out Words

At work time, Ellen draws a picture, shows it to Rosie, her teacher, and tells her about the basket she has drawn. At the end of the conversation, Rosie asks Ellen if she would write her name on the picture so other children will know it's hers. Ellen takes a sticky note from Rosie's pocket and writes *ELLEN*. Then, on another sticky, she writes *BASKAT*, making the sound of each letter as she writes it.

Identify and Search for Letters by Their Sounds

126. **At snack time.** Serve alphabet pretzels at snack time. As you eat a pretzel, comment on its letter sound. For example, as you pick up a *B* pretzel you might say

"I'm eating a letter that makes the /b/ sound. I'm eating the letter *B!*" or "I'm eating a letter that makes the /m/ sound like the first letter of Mia's name. I'm eating the letter *M.*"

As children catch on, you might say

> "Next I think I'll eat a letter that makes the /s/ sound. What letter do you think I'll eat next that makes the /s/ sound?"

Be on the look out for children to take over your role as the leader in this game.

127. At small-group time. Give each child some clay or dough. Set out, where the children can easily see and reach them, a large selection of three-dimensional letters with enough duplicate letters to allow each child to find the specified letters. Then go on a letter hunt. For example, you might say

> "Let's go on a letter hunt. Can you find a letter that makes the /m/ sound and put it in your dough?"

You might also say

> "Look for a letter that makes a sound in your name."

Be on the lookout for children to take over your role as the leader in this game. After you've gone through three or four letters, review the sounds of the letters selected and look at what children have done with their letters and dough.

"I know where that /o/ sound is," Jamal says. He points to the O's in "whooooo" and says the O's again, "/o/!"

128. At clean-up time. When you and the children are cleaning up after a work time or small-group time involving three-dimensional letters or letter tiles, challenge children to find letters by sound. For example, you might say

> "Let's put away all the letters that make the /b/ sound."

Ask the children for a letter sound to search for.

129. In alphabet books. At snack or small-group time, read a familiar alphabet book that includes a picture and a printed word for each picture—for example, the first page includes the letter *A*, a picture of an ape, and the printed word *Ape*. Instead of just saying the letter, say the sound it makes. For example, you might read

> "*A* makes the sound /ā/ for the first letter in *ape*. *B* makes the sound /b/ for the first letter in *buffalo*. *C* makes the sound /k/ for the first letter in *cat…*"

Adjust the letter sound to fit the picture. For example, for the picture of an eagle you would say

"E makes the sound /ē/ for the first letter in eagle."

But for the picture of an elephant you would say

"E makes the sound /ĕ/ for the first letter in elephant."

Represent Sounds With Letters

130. At small-group time, animal sounds. Draw a snake, make a snake's hissing sound, ask the children for letters to use to write down the sound, and write the suggested letters on your snake picture. Then, give each child drawing materials. Ask the children to draw an animal and write the sound their animal makes, using letters they know to stand for the animal's sound. Talk with children about their work and make note of the sound-letter connections the children make. For example, if a child draws a bee and writes a line of *Z*'s you might say

"Tell me about your animal and the sound it makes." If the child says it's a bee that goes *buzzzz*, you might say "I see you made lots of *Z*'s for the *zzzzz* sound the bee makes."

If a child draws a dog and writes some *F*'s for *woof* you might say

"I see that you wrote a lot of *F*'s for the /f/ sound at the end of *woof*—woofffffff."

If a child draws a bird and writes *FP* for *flap* you might say

> "You wrote an *F* for the /f/ sound at the beginning of *flap* and a *P* for the /p/ sound at the end of *flap.*"

If a child draws an animal but writes no letters, you might say

> "Tell me about your animal." If the child says it's a goldfish that doesn't make any sound, you might say "I've never heard a goldfish make any sound either!"

*Serena looks for the /s/ sound in the word **octopus**. "It's like the /s/ sound in my name!" she says.*

HELPFUL
RESOURCES

MATERIALS LIST

1. **Materials for Identifying Sounds**

   Everyday sound-making materials: for example, wooden blocks, chopsticks, tin cans, metal spoons, keys, paper plates, cellophane, newspaper

   Percussion instruments: shakers, drums, bells, tambourines, triangles, wood blocks, and clavés

   Xylophones and mallets

   Tape player and tapes or CD player and CDs: for example, bird calls, waterfalls, chimes

   Tape recorder and blank tape

   Camera

   Toy animal sets

   Animal photos and/or pictures

   Set of identical boxes or small containers

   Ticking clock or timer

2. **Materials for Building Rhyme Awareness**

   Rhyme and poem collections (see "Sample Rhyme and Poem Collections" on page 20)

   Rhyming story books (see "Sample Rhyming Stories" on page 20")

   Rhyming song books (see "Sample Rhyming Song Books" on page 22)

   Sets of objects with rhyming names (see list on page 26, Activity 44)

   Puppets

When print materials, letter sets, and writing tools are a familiar part of the classroom, children enjoy trying out writing for themselves.

3. **Materials for Building Alliteration Awareness**

   Stories and rhymes that include alliteration (see "Sample Storybooks That Include Alliteration" on page 34)

   Sets of objects with alliterative names (see list on pages 37–38)

4. **Materials for Recognizing Letters**

Drawing and writing tools, paper

Writing materials related to play (see list on page 41, Activity 82)

Sidewalk chalk

Envelopes

Sets of three-dimensional letters, one set per child

Alphabet puzzles

Alphabet pretzels

Clay, dough, wire, pipe cleaners, sand

Typewriters

Letter stamps and ink pads

Optional: computers, children's word-processing and drawing programs

Letter blocks, cards, and tiles

Alphabet books (see "Sample Alphabet Books" on page 48)

Camera

Photographs of children

Newspapers, magazines, food labels, scissors

5. **Materials for Building Letter-Sound Awareness**

Drawing and writing tools, paper

Sets of letter blocks

Toy animals

Sets of magnetic letters and metal trays (cookie sheets)

Erase boards and markers

Letter stickers

Alphabet pretzels

Clay or dough

Three-dimensional letters

Alphabet books (see "Sample Alphabet Books" on page 48)

ACTIVITY LOG

Explore Sound-Making Materials

1.	Everyday materials			
2.	Outside materials			
3.	Percussion instruments			
4.	Xylophones			

Attend to Environmental Sounds

5.	Sounds you hear			
6.	Sounds children hear			

Identify Rest-Time Sounds

7.	Indoor sounds			
8.	Outdoor sounds			
9.	Taped sounds			

Identify Snack- or Meal-Time Sounds

10.	While eating			
11.	Before eating			

Identify Sounds on a Walk

12.	Listening for sounds			
13.	Listening for and taping sounds			

Identify Animal Sounds

14.	Live animals			
15.	Animal photos			
16.	Toy animals at planning			
17.	Toy animals at recall			
18.	Animal photos at planning and recall			
19.	Made-up animal sounds			

Locate Sounds

20.	At planning/recall, finding the noisy box			
21.	At recall time, finding the ticking clock			

Identify Voices

22.	Work-time voices			
23.	Outside-time voices			
24.	Field-trip voices			

Listen for a Word or Phrase

25.	One magic word			
26.	One magic word from a child			
27.	One magic word repeated twice			
28.	Two magic words			

Repertoire of Rhymes, Rhyming Songs, and Stories

29.	Rhymes and poems			
30.	Rhyming stories			
31.	Rhyming songs			

Identify Rhyming Words

32.	Using the word *rhyme* while reading stories			
33.	Children finding rhymes			

Fill in the Missing Rhyme

34.	One missing rhyme			
35.	Two missing rhymes			

Substitute Nonrhyming Words

36.	One new nonrhyming word			
37.	New nonrhyming words from children			

Substitute New Rhymes for Old

38.	New rhyming words			
39.	New rhyming words from children			

[This is a reproducible page.]

Do It When It Rhymes

40.	Name-and-word pairs		
41.	Name-and-word pairs from children		
42.	Three pairs of words, all words different		
43.	Word-pair variations		

Find Objects With Rhyming Names

44.	One object		
45.	Two objects		
46.	Room search		
47.	Guessing objects with rhyming names		
48.	Cleanup "I Spy"		
49.	Snack-time "I Spy"		
50.	Child-led "I Spy"		

Make Up Rhymes

51.	Guessing what rhymes with...		
52.	Rhyming puppet names, planning		
53.	Rhyming puppet names, recall		
54.	Name rhymes		
55.	Outdoor rhymes		
56.	Food rhymes		

Look for Rhyming Pictures

57.	In storybooks at snack		
58.	In storybooks at greeting circle		
59.	In storybooks at small-group time		
60.	In the *I Spy* books		

Build Rhymes From Rhyme Endings

61.	Guessing what rhymes with -ack		
62.	Thinking of words that end with -ate.		

Build an Alliteration Repertoire

63.	Alliterative phrases in stories, rhymes, songs		
64.	Alliterative phrases in everyday conversation		

Identify Alliterations

65.	Pointing out common beginning sounds		
66.	Using the word *alliteration*		

Fill in the Missing Alliterations

67.	Alliterative phrases from children		

Substitute New Alliterations for Old

68.	Replacing the first sound (initial phoneme)		
69.	New first sounds (initial phonemes) from children		

Do It When You Hear the Alliteration

70.	Name-based alliterations		
71.	Name-based alliterations from children		

Tell Stories about Alliterative Objects

72.	Individual stories		
73.	Group stories		
74.	Stories from pictures		

Play Alliterative "I Spy"

75.	At snack time		
76.	At cleanup time		
77.	At recall time		
78.	Recall-time variation		

Make Up Name-Based Alliterations

79.	At greeting circle		
80.	At snack or meal time		

Draw, Scribble, and Write Letters

81.	At work time		
82.	During pretend play		
83.	At outside time		
84.	At planning time		
85.	At recall time		
86.	At small-group time, cards		
87.	At small-group time, more cards		
88.	After a field trip		

[This is a reproducible page.]

Identify Three-Dimensional Letters

89. At work time			
90. At small-group time, 12 letters			
91. At small-group time, known/unknown letters			
92. At small-group time, letters in name			
93. At small-group time, alphabet puzzles			
94. At snack time, alphabet pretzels			

Make Three-Dimensional Letters

95. At small-group time, clay or dough			
96. At small-group time, wire			
97. At small-group time, pipe cleaners			
98. At small-group time, sand			

Type and Print Letters

99. At work time			
100. At small-group time, computers			
101. At small-group time, letter stamps			

Sort and Arrange Letter Blocks, Tiles, and Cards

102. At work time			
103. At small-group time, letters for each child			
104. At small-group time, letter search, blocks/tiles			
105. At small-group time, letter search with cards			

Identify Letters in Print

106. At snack time			
107. At small-group time, making alphabet books			
108. At small-group, name-based alphabet books			
109. At small-group time, identifying outdoor print			
110. At small-group time, cutting out letters			
111. At small-group time, using cut-out letters			

Sound Out Letter Strings and Combinations

112. At work time			
113. At small-group time, random-letter trains			
114. At small-group time, selected-letter trains			
115. At small-group time, letters-in-name trains			
116. At small-group time, random-letter fences			

Connect Sounds to Letters Children Use

117. At work time			
118. At small-group time, magnetic letters			
119. At small-group time, erase board			
120. At small-group time, letter stickers			

Link Letter Sounds/Names When Spelling

121. Beginning and ending sounds in words			
122. Remaining sounds in words			
123. At planning time, words and pictures			
124. At recall time, words and pictures			
125. At snack, food words			

Identify and Search for Letters by Their Sounds

126. At snack time			
127. At small-group time			
128. At cleanup time			
129. In alphabet books			

Represent Sounds With Letters

130. At small-group time, animal sounds			

[This is a reproducible page.]

ASSESSING LITERACY DEVELOPMENT

The language and literacy items from High/Scope's child assessment instrument, the **High/Scope Child Observation Record for Ages 2½–6,** can be used, in conjunction with the activities in this book, to gauge children's progress:

As children carry out an activity, watch and listen to them closely. Jot quick notes to yourself. Organize your notes into brief factual anecdotes. Use these anecdotes to keep track of each child's level of language and literacy development using the items from the High/Scope COR as a reference point. For more about the COR or to order a complete copy, go to the High/Scope Web Site (*www.highscope.org*). Following are the language and literacy items from COR Versions A (1992 edition) and B (revised edition, currently under development).

Version A COR Items

Item Q. Understanding speech

Level 1   Child seldom responds when spoken to by others.

Level 2   Child follows simple directions ("Come to the circle").

Level 3   Child responds to simple, direct, conversational sentences.

Level 4   Child participates in ordinary classroom conversation.

Level 5   Child follows multistep or complex directions.

Item R. Speaking

Level 1   Child does not yet speak or uses only a few one- or two-word phrases.

Level 2   Child uses simple sentences of more than two words.

Level 3   Child uses sentences that include two or more separate ideas.

Level 4   Child uses sentences that include two or more ideas with descriptive details ("I stacked up the red blocks too high and they fell down").

Level 5   Child makes up and tells well-developed, detailed stories, rhymes, or songs.

Item S. Showing interest in reading activities

Level 1   Child does not yet show interest in reading activities.

Level 2   Child shows interest when stories are read.

Level 3   Child asks people to read stories, signs, or notes.

Level 4   Child answers questions about a story that has been read or repeats part of a story.

Level 5   Child often reads a book or tells a story while turning the pages.

Item T. Demonstrating knowledge about books

Level 1   Child does not yet pick up books and hold them conventionally.

Level 2   Child picks up books and holds them conventionally, looking at the pages and turning them.

Level 3   Child picture-reads, telling the story from the pictures on the cover or in the book.

Level 4   Child follows the print on a page, moving his or her eyes in the correct direction (usually left to right and top to bottom).

Level 5   Child appears to read or actually reads a book, pointing to the words and telling the story.

Item U. Beginning reading

Level 1   Child does not yet identify letters or numbers.

Level 2   Child identifies some letters and numbers.

Level 3   Child reads several words, or a few simple phrases or sentences ("I love Mom").

Level 4   Child reads a variety of sentences.

Level 5   Child reads simple stories or books.

Item V. Beginning writing

Level 1   Child does not yet attempt to write.

Level 2   Child writes using squiggles and marks as letters.

Level 3   Child copies or writes identifiable letters, perhaps including own name.

Level 4   Child writes some words or short phrases besides own name.

Level 5   Child writes a variety of phrases or sentences.

Version B COR Items

Item Q. Listening to and understanding speech

Level 1   Child responds with actions or words to a suggestion, request, or question.

Level 2   When listening to a story, rhyme, or narrative, child anticipates and fills in a word or phrase.

Level 3   When listening to a story, rhyme, or narrative, child comments on or asks a question about it.

Level 4   Child contributes to an ongoing conversation.

Level 5   Child sustains a dialogue, taking three or more conversational turns.

Item R. Using words to communicate

Level 1   Child talks about people or objects close at hand.

Level 2   Child talks about absent people or objects.

Level 3   Child uses vocabulary related to a particular subject.

Level 4   Child uses two or more descriptive words to describe something.

Level 5   Child asks about the meaning of a word.

Item S. Using complex patterns of speech

Level 1   Child uses words and phrases.

Level 2   Child uses a sentence of four or more words.

Level 3   Child uses two or more simple sentences in a row.

Level 4   Child uses a compound subject or object in a sentence.

Level 5   Child uses a clause that starts with "when," "if," "because," or "since" in a sentence.

Item T. Showing awareness of word sounds

Level 1   During play, child makes the sound of an animal or vehicle, or some other environmental sound.

Level 2   Child joins in saying or repeats a rhyme or a series of words that start with the same sound.

Level 3   Child rhymes one word with another or makes up a phrase or sentence that includes a rhyme.

Level 4   Child says that two words begin with the same sound.

Level 5   Child creates a pair or series of words that start with the same sound.

Item U. Demonstrating knowledge about books

Level 1   Child shows interest when a book is read aloud.

Level 2   Child holds a book right-side up, turns the pages, and looks at them.

Level 3   Child asks another person to read a book to him or her.

Level 4   Looking at the pictures in a book, child tells the story or makes up a story related to the pictures.

Level 5   Child points to the words in a book or follows a line of text while telling or reading the story.

Item V. Using letter names and sounds

Level 1   Child says or sings some letters.

Level 2   Child names three or more alphabet letters he or she is holding, looking at, typing, or making.

Level 3   Child makes the sound of a letter in a word he or she is looking at, writing, or typing.

Level 4   Child names 10 or more letters over time.

Level 5   Child says a word and identifies the beginning letter or sound.

Item W. Reading

Level 1   Child uses the same word to name more than one object.

Level 2   Child says what a picture or symbol refers to.

Level 3   Child calls attention to print.

Level 4   Child recognizes a written word.

Level 5   Child reads aloud a simple phrase or sentence.

Item X. Writing

Level 1   Child writes using pictures, squiggles, or letterlike forms.

Level 2   Child uses a material like clay, wire, or sticks to make a recognizable letter.

Level 3   Child writes two or more recognizable letters.

Level 4   Child writes a string of letters and reads them or asks to have them read.

Level 5   Child writes a phrase or sentence of two or more words.

Phonics Fact Sheet for Parents

Phonics is in the news! Here are some phonics-related facts and concepts that will help you understand the developing abilities of your preschool-aged child:

Hearing the Sounds That Make Up Words

Phonics helps children in kindergarten, first, and second grade as they learn to read. As is true in many areas of academic learning, the ability to learn and use phonics in the early grades depends on skills and abilities children begin to develop before they enter grade school:

- Phonics involves the relationship between printed letters and the sounds they stand for. (The letter *B* corresponds to the sound /b/).

- To understand these letter-sound relationships, children first need to develop awareness of the sounds that make up words. This is called *phonological awareness.*

- Learning and using phonics depends on children's ability to hear *phonemes,* the very smallest sounds in words. Phonemes are represented in print by single letters (the letter *t* stands for the sound /t/) or, in some cases, by letter combinations (the letters *sh* stand for the sound /sh/; the letters *ck* stand for the sound /k/).

How Preschool Phonics Learning Begins: Rhyming, Alliteration, and Writing

- While preschoolers are not able to distinguish all the phonemes in the words they hear and say, they can hear and identify the ends of words that sound the same, for example, d**og**, l**og**, b**og.** These are commonly known as *rhymes.* They are also able to distinguish the beginning phonemes of words that begin with the same sound, for example, **T**om **T**it **T**ot. These are called *alliterations.*

- As preschool children hear and say familiar nursery rhymes, pick out the rhyming words, and make up their own rhymes, they distinguish and purposefully play with word-ending sounds.

- As preschool children say, hear, and make up alliterations, they distinguish beginning letter sounds, a skill necessary for learning phonics.

- As preschool children begin to sound out and write letters in familiar words (saying /m/ as they write the letter *M* for *MOM),* they use phonics (letter-sound relationships) to help them spell.

Since experiences like these with rhyming, alliteration, and writing are a frequent part of our active learning preschool program, you can be assured that your child is getting the phonics-related activities she or he needs! ◆

About the Author

Mary Hohmann, a staff member of the High/Scope Foundation since 1970, has served as a High/Scope preschool teacher, curriculum trainer, and writer, and as an educational consultant in the United States and in other countries. Mary is coauthor of High/Scope's preschool manual, *Educating Young Children: Active Learning Practices for Preschool and Child Care Programs,* author of *A Study Guide to Educating Young Children: Exercises for Adult Learners,* and coauthor of High/Scope's infant-toddler manual, *Tender Care and Early Learning: Supporting Infants and Toddlers in Child Care Settings.* Mary is also one of the developers of the High/Scope Child Observation Record (COR) assessment instrument (infant-toddler and preschool versions).